CONTEMPORARY CRAFTS
FOR THE HOME

Bill Kraus, *Author*
Toni Fountain Sikes, *Editor*

KRAUS SIKES INC.

CONTEMPORARY CRAFTS
FOR THE HOME

FEATURING WINNERS OF THE AMERICAN CRAFTS AWARDS

Published by:
Kraus Sikes Inc.
1232 Madison Avenue
New York, NY 10128
(212) 410-4110

ISBN 0-935603-18-2

Distributed by:
U.S. Book Trade Publication:
North Light, an imprint of Writer's Digest Books
1507 Dana Avenue
Cincinnati, OH 45207
(513) 531-2222

Distributed outside of the U.S.A. and Canada by:
Hearst Books International
105 Madison Avenue
New York, NY 10016

Title Page: 2″ square stoneware tiles for fireplace border by Barbara
Archer/Barry Rhodes. Photo © 1988 Bard Wrisley.

Contents Page: (top left) "The House Chair" by Anderson/Schwartz; (top right)
stair railing by Chris Hughes; (bottom left) hand-painted silk charmeuse jacquard
by Sissi Siska; (bottom right) "American Krishna" by Thomas McCanna.

Page 6: forged stair railing by David A. Ponsler.

Color separations, printing and binding by Mandarin Offset.
Book design and composition by The Sarabande Press.

Printed in Hong Kong.

CONTENTS

FOREWORD

AS I WRITE THESE WORDS, MY MIND IS DRIFTING TO THE GRANITE-bounded coast of Maine where I will be in two days, and where my family and I have just finished building and furnishing a winterized summer home.

Even as I sit here, 500 miles away, I can walk through every room, brush my hand over the glossy surface of craftsman Joe Tracy's dining room table, sit in contemplation of stone artist Jeff Gammelin's monumental granite fireplace, or steam the seaward windows while gazing across landscaper Pat Chasse's undulating stone terrace.

These three craftsmen were the core of a team I assembled to bring texture to a dream house which Robert Venturi would design and which would incorporate much of the natural surrounding stone and wood in its interior details.

Because from the very outset I was involved in selecting the artists and artisans and then oversaw the evolution of a million details, it is not a difficult task to sit in my Manhattan office and simultaneously prowl the painted maple floors of a shingle house in Maine. And the process was as exciting as the result. Learning to trust one's own amateur instincts, daring to disagree with a master and—equally—daring to trust that someone else's eccentric vision would somehow fit.

It would all have been different if this had been an "instant house" project: you know, just add money and stir. A house can be such a subtle manifestation of personal style and taste, but only if the client is intimately involved in thinking how he wants to live, sharing with others that vision, and then commenting actively on the artistic responses as they evolve.

Our first house warming event was held for the two hundred people who helped to build our dream. At the door we greeted each contributor with a special name tag attached to a slice of red cedar shingle. The tags read, "Joe Tracy—wood," "Jeff Gammelin—stone," etc. My young daughters' subscripts read "demolition." Many craftsmen brought their spouses and inevitably guided them to their own handrail or counter top or cabinet door. It was overwhelming to think how much loving labor had gone into producing our home, and the sense of painstaking love is what persists so happily for us today.

I wish each reader of this fine book the same joy in crafting a home of his or her own.

David Rockefeller, Jr.

CONTEMPORARY CRAFTS
FOR THE HOME

PERSONAL SIGNATURES

NOT ONLY CAN YOU GO HOME AGAIN, YOU DO go home again—and again and again. More and more people are doing just that. As Americans search for a sanctuary in this fast-paced world, we are looking homeward to find it. The home has taken on a new significance as we are spending increasing amounts of time there—enjoying family, entertaining friends, sometimes working, and often just relaxing.

The home seems to be providing something beyond being a simple refuge; it is the place that we can make a footprint, put our stamp, inscribe our personal signature. The home is a singular place now as we put more time, energy, and money into personalizing it.

The industrial revolution and mass production brought good things to many people as factories poured out an enormous variety of consumer goods at affordable prices, but it was not an unalloyed blessing. We paid a price for its contributions. It gave us a kind of a cookie-cutter world where variety was sacrificed to the efficiencies that attend making many copies of the same

Hand-crafted work inscribes its own personal signature. Sherry Schreiber's landscape tapestry (top) in an Adirondack-inspired home, Chris Hughes' railing (bottom left), Rodger Reid's pine library (bottom center), and Gregg Lipton's queen size bed and side table all individualize the spaces they occupy.

This page: Ayalah Sorkin "signs" her vibrantly colored rug entitled "Celebration" (top). It is 6' × 9' and hand-tufted of 100% wool pile. "Whoops," the glass art painting over the bed (right) by Nancy Gong is made of sheet glass which has been etched, carved, and painted with lead accents.

Opposite page: Gregg Lipton's standing mirror (top) is on a satinwood and purpleheart frame. The clock by Todd Noe (bottom) is on a bed of plate glass with a nickel plated, brass core for the quartz movement.

thing. What we are seeing now is counter-revolution to the industrial revolution.

If keeping up with the Joneses was a benchmark of the style imposed by mass production—where our ambition was to have exactly what our neighbor had—what we are now seeing is something more introspective. The Joneses are fine, and they should do their thing to their heart's content. But each of us has different, complicated psychic needs and tastes. So now what we do is look inward first, instead of looking next door, and then build an environment for what we find when we look at ourselves.

One of the major manifestations of this counter-movement has been a return to the crafts world for things that are products of the head and the hand and the heart, objects that are unique, work that bears the personal signature of the artist. The evident presence of the human hand draws us back to values believed to be lost, as we turn away from the trendy in search of the enduring. We have re-discovered the love of materials, the joy of singularity, the pleasure of a thing well made.

This has been a boon to the crafts field, reminiscent of the Arts and Crafts movement at the turn of the century. It has brought increased recognition to those artists who have been working quietly on the sidelines for so long. Today, a growing nucleus of artists and artisans are creating exciting products for our homes. They are producing work that is made of traditional materials using traditional techniques as well as pieces crafted in unexpected ways with innovative materials.

———————

As the search for personalization of the home has become widespread, contemporary craft artists are available and ready to fill the burgeoning demand for the unusual, the commissioned, the unique, and the hand-crafted. Their work can be purchased through galleries, retail shops, and the growing number of home furnishing stores that specialize in things unique. Artists will often sell their work directly too, either at craft fairs or right out of their studios.

There are many reasons for this placement of signatures in the places where we live. The most important is that our living spaces are being designed and crafted with the goal of articulating a personality rather than a pre-ordained, systematic decorating style. The "combination" living room—

sofa, love seat, coffeetable and matching end tables—is becoming extinct as people learn to express themselves through the rooms of their homes. Today's homes speak chapters, if not volumes, about someone's life style. People are becoming more self-confident about their own tastes, and somewhat more assertive as well one suspects.

No longer do you traverse a suburban neighborhood and go from predictable house to predictable house and find that each of them is full of straw wallpaper and beige carpets and barrel chairs. The time when the owners dared to choose their favorite colors and not much more seems to be safely behind us. A new design spirit has liberated us.

Mismatching and eclecticism are not only permitted, they are even encouraged. The soul is not beige, after all. It is more a Joseph's coat. We are diverse, paradoxical, often contradictory creatures. We are not colorcoordinated, and we are finding a renewed delight in creating and living in places that are as variable and surprising and unpredictable as we are. The signature home is likely to have an English antique desk in the same room with a new wave sofa. Flea market finds sit comfortably side by side with pieces purchased at galleries. And crafts are everywhere.

You are likely to see crafted objects all over the house, dominating a room

Juan and Patricia Navarrete hand build site specific fireplaces. This 9' × 12' freestanding fireplace (left) was made of gypsum plaster. Dale Zheutlin's "Cycloid" (top) is the only curve in a house full of horizontal and vertical elements. The translucent porcelain light column (bottom) by Curtis and Suzan Benzle illuminates and beautifies the room it graces.

This page: "Kneeling Woman," bronze candleholders (top left) by Chris Wilson; silk throw designed by Anne Lanford Dalton (top right); "Terracotta Collage," a hand painted bedcover by Jill Wilcox (bottom left); Andrea Serafino's 4' × 7' carpet (bottom right).

Opposite page: Wooden cooking and serving utensils by Gerald Ulrich (top); Paula Bowers' hand dyed wool wall hanging above bed (bottom left); Rosanne Somerson's prize winning couch/daybed (bottom right).

or providing a vital imaginative detail. There are the hand-carved wooden spoons, the woven throw on the sofa, the quilt on the bed, and the wall hanging over it. Even the brass candlesticks on the dining room table are more than likely the signed product of some craft artist whose taste and sensibilities match those of the owner of the home you are visiting.

The artist who conspires to help us find our own personal style is also saying, "use my art." The hand-woven rug is, of course, beautiful and beautifully made and could be hung on the wall and viewed as a painting. But the rug was made to be used, to be walked on, and to soothe tired feet; it invites us to sit on it with friends, to wrestle on it with grandchildren. This rug becomes an active part of our lives. It's beautiful, but its beauty enhances rather than interferes with its function.

The craft artist who was once relegated to the backwoods is suddenly back in the mainstream, if not the forefront of designs for the home. If

"The Ort Rug" created by Arlyn Ende
is hooked, tufted, and sculpted wool.
It is 15′ 8″ × 9′ 6″ and was
commissioned by Alice Zimmerman
and Sanford Ross for the dining room
of their home in Nashville, Tennessee.
This colorful and amusing rug has
scattered dining fragments sculpted
into the rug; diners who slip off their
shoes get an extra treat for the feet!

diversity is what we seek, we have only to look to the thousands of craft artists who are in their studios weaving, throwing pots, blowing glass, shaping metal, carving and sanding wood—waiting for the world to discover the unique and often astonishing things they are creating to express themselves and us as well.

The craft artists of this country are, metaphorically at least, stocking a veritable "Alice's Restaurant" for us. It is inconceivable that there is not an artist out there for every taste, for every need, for every home, for every niche in every home. They were there while the world of design was homogenizing, and they are still there. And now they are back in demand, because more and more of us want them and their work. Anonymity angst seems to be passing. Keeping up with the Joneses may not be entirely passe, but being just like the Joneses certainly is. We no longer seek the safety of sameness.

We are regaining our senses and our humanity. And we are making homes that fit us, that suit us, that reflect us. Our homes are hand-crafted and signed. What we seem to be saying is "This is not just mine. This is me."

Al Garvey's door (top) is designed to reflect the architectural elements of a home. The forged stair railing by David A. Ponsler (bottom) graces this entry.

The "Blue Room" built-ins and trim are made from maple and cherry with bubinga and ebony inlay; they and the bookcase and mantel are the work of Thomas J. Beck.

FOR THE TABLE

THE TABLE IS THE CENTER OF EVERY HOME, the ultimate gathering place. It is where family and friends come together to eat, of course, but also to celebrate the ritualistic dates and events in our lives. It is fitting that as the table regains its rightful place of eminence in our homes that we can find craft artists who are dressing up the table top, as well as the food and drink served there.

Today's artists have created a cornucopia of beautiful, useful objects for the table. There are aluminum salt and pepper shakers, ceramic coffee cups, wooden cooking utensils that fit the hand and please the eye. You can find a fanciful cake server made of precious materials that cuts the cake, and also graces the platter and the occasion too somehow.

There is handmade dinnerware that has the look and feel of museum pieces but is dishwasher safe and does not require that you take out a second mortgage to buy the requisite number of place settings. The dinnerware crosses and recrosses the line between the artful and the practical. You don't have to choose between art and utility, which, of course, is the idea.

The use of contemporary materials for traditional objects is widespread. But the heirloom candidates are

The nasturtium dining set (top) includes etched glass by Kathy Barnard and sterling flatware by Robin Nichols; Thomas Seabury Brown's set of four goblets (bottom left) are anodized aluminum and 18K gold plated brass. Neophile's fruit platter (bottom center) is made of handpainted wood and etched glass and measures 18″ × 8″. The porcelain teapot and cup (bottom right) are by Jinny De Paul. All are examples of handcrafted work that brings life and individuality to a table.

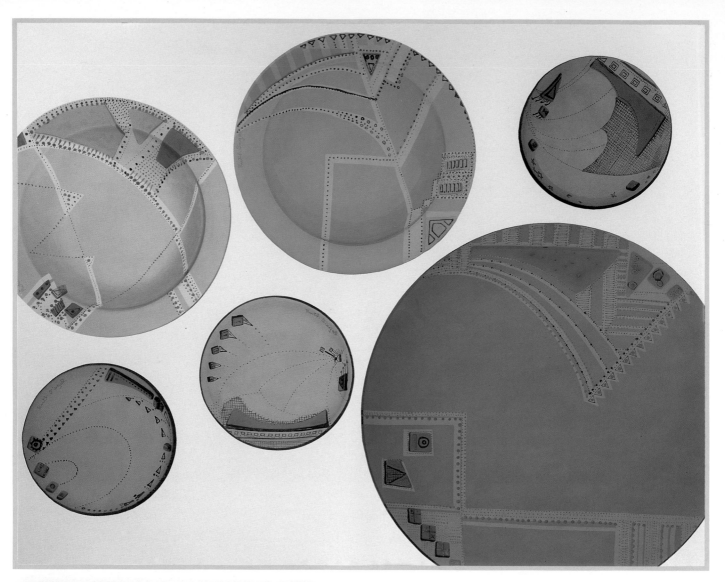

Ruth Siegel's glass service plates (top) range from a few inches to 18 inches. Each dish is fused, decorated with gold luster and enamels, then the design is slumped into a mold. Taylor Backes' watermelon bowl (bottom) is 10″ in diameter and 5″ high and is handblown glass.

also alive and well. If you don't think the butter dish made of industrial glass will be in your grandchildren's cabinet, you can be pretty sure that the silver coffee server will.

One gets an almost subliminal sense of the luxurious from the heft of a hand-thrown, earthenware salad bowl, which is like the other seven bowls in the set, but not exactly, and which has not only its own distinctive look but its own feel as well.

The contemporary craft artists who are re-creating our tables, our gathering places, are showing us that function can be, should be an artful blend of utility and beauty. It is not enough that the objects we use at the tables where we eat and meet do the things they are intended to do. They should have some character and spirit as well—they should be a reflection of the people who use them.

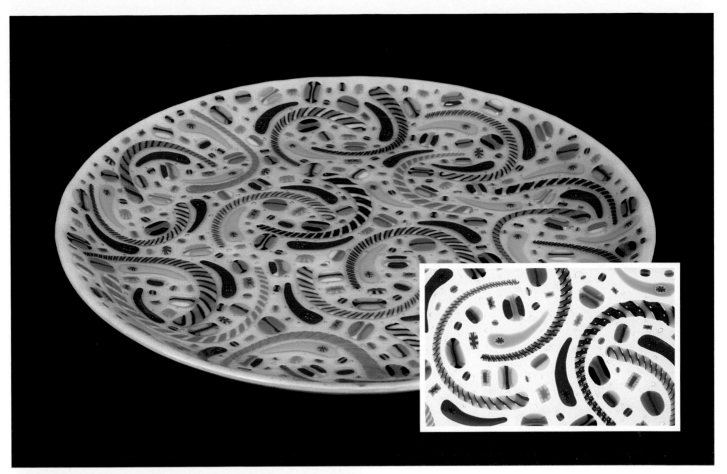

Artists working in glass are turning to dinnerware with a vengeance. Jesse Gregg's glass platter (top) is 17½" in diameter and ¼" thick. Gregg fuses and slumps his glass pieces, incorporating hot worked elements to create a swirling world of bright colors.
The black glass platter is 3" high and 21" in diameter (middle photo). Glass artist Robert Toensing crystal etches his work to create intricate patterns.
Ann Morhauser's glass plate and place setting (bottom photos) are limited edition pieces she did for Annieglass Studio. The sizes range from 5" to 14"; each plate is enameled, slumped, and polished.

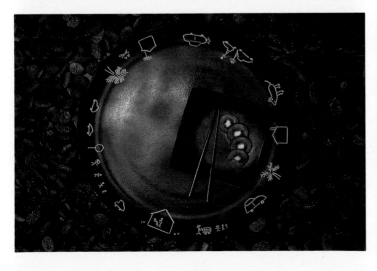

Mesolini Glass Studio creates dishware from handmade iridescent glass; the dishes are both practical and aesthetically pleasing. Photo by Bob Michels; usage rights courtesy of the California Artichoke Advisory Board.

Stanley Mace Andersen's pitcher, plate, cups, and saucers (top photos) are of earthenware clay decorated with the majolica technique. The "Ijabo Platters" (middle) measure 31" × 13" × 5" each and are by Claudia Reese. Georgina Holt's porcelain slab-built pitchers (bottom) range from 9½" to 5½" high. The porcelain dinnerware (inset, bottom) is dishwasher and microwave safe because of high-firing with a gloss glaze. Each piece is one-of-a-kind and individually made.

Joseph A. Triplo's place setting is high-fired, hand made porcelain. Everything is dishwasher safe and oven proof. The dinner plate is 11¾", the cake plate is 7¾", the bowls are 7½", the saucer is 4", and the cups are 3" high. The beauty of the Japanese influence is heightened by the contrast with the rough setting.

Mara Superior's 17" × 24" porcelain vessel (top) is titled "Piscatorial Imaginings." Both sides of the piece are pictured, each telling its own story of the sea. The serving platters and goblet by Don Drumm (bottom) are cast aluminum alloy. They are hand finished and polished and part of the artist's "cooking sculpture" repertoire.

Carol and Jean-Pierre Hsu make these anodized aluminum bowls for the table in every imaginable, eye-catching color. They are 11½" in diameter and 6" tall and come with matching salad servers.

Marion Grant's "Postcards" (top) are made with textile watercolor and pearlescent pigments on cotton sateen. The set includes tablecloth, placemats, and napkins. The "Tropic Wave" teapot set with matching dinnerware (bottom) is by ceramist Valerie Hoh.

Susan Bankert combines utility, spontaneity, and elegance in her work. Her clay pitcher (top left) is 12" high and comes with matching tumblers. The pitcher and tumbler (bottom) are made of slip-cast earthenware by Michael Lamar and Gibb Brownlie under the Butter + Toast label. Kathryn Berd makes her red earthenware cups and saucers (top right) with slips and underglazes.

Women artists who are designing and creating contemporary table top objects using traditional silversmithing techniques include Randy Long and Susan Ewing.

This page: Randy Long's "Minoan Coffee Server" (bottom) is 9½" × 8½" × 2¾" and is made of sterling silver and 18K gold; the "Hsing Teapot" (top) by Long uses the same materials and has a purple heartwood handle.

Opposite page: Susan Ewing's "Vessel with Golden Light" is made of sterling silver with 24K gold vermeil. It is 4½" high.

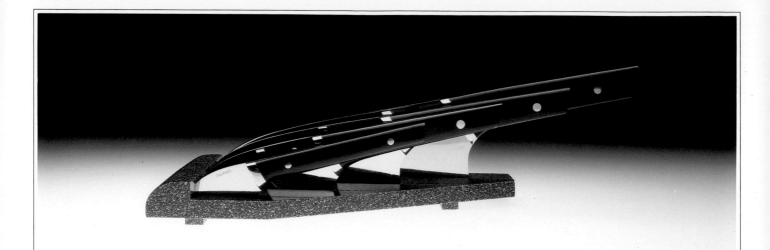

Artists are mixing media, using old and new materials, when forging flatware. Joseph DiGangi's four piece cutlery set with handground blades (top) have black micarta handles and are in a corian stand. "Tablewear" by Boris Bally (right) marries ebony wood handles with gleaming, textured silver. Robyn Nichols made the watermelon leaf servers (bottom left) of sterling silver. The slotted spoon and pastry set are each 10" long. Mardi-Jo Cohen's cake cutter (bottom middle) has a companion, an equally whimsical ice cream server (bottom right). Cohen mixes silver, pearl, acrylic, and color core in her work.

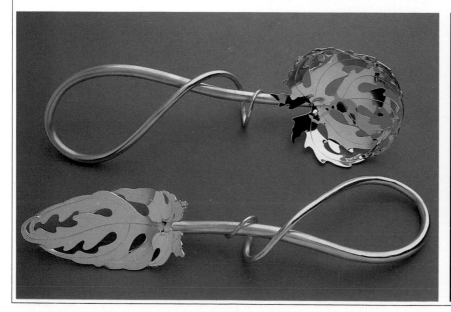

Skip Gaynard's hand forged sterling silver and 14K gold napkin rings (top photos) are 7" long. The hand-printed tablecloth and napkins (center) are by Marion Grant. Sam Farmer calls these "Napkin Rings for Lovers" (bottom).

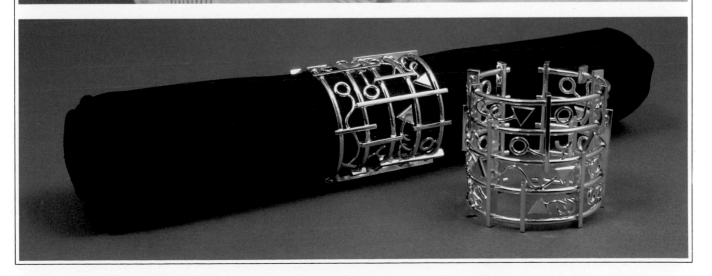

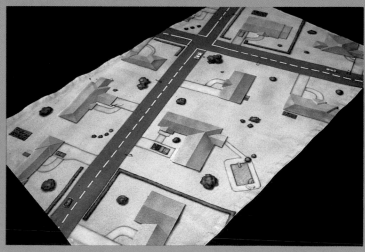

FOR THE FLOOR

A FLOOR IS A FLOOR IS A FLOOR. THAT IS, UN-til you begin to think of it as something more than a floor. When you think of the floor as a wall, perhaps you think of it a little differently. It is still something to walk on instead of lean against, but it is something to look at as well. It is part of the room, it contributes to the look of the room. It is no longer just a bland background on which furniture and objects reside.

Once you decide that the floor is not merely an unobtrusive background for rooms and the lives lived in those rooms, a whole new world of possibilities opens up.

In the beginning there were rugs. These woven floor coverings have a rich history of serving as items of comfort and symbols of status for the pharaohs, for royalty, even for the pilgrims.

The contemporary version of yesterday's oriental rug decorates the floor as well as covers it. Today's fiber artists weave their creative ideas into art for the bottom of the room.

The weaver's artistic sensibilities range from the colorful and exotic, to the abstract geometric, to subtle elegance. Variety of style is matched by variety of techniques. These rugs are hooked, tufted, sheared, sculp-

The 10′ × 10′, 100% wool rug by Francis Sanders (top photo) was woven in four separate panels and pieced together. The detail shot (bottom right) is also of a Sanders rug, of cotton chenille and linen. Gabriel L. Romeu's "Broken Column Floorcloth" (bottom left) and the entry hall with wood marquetry and an oak border (bottom center) by Lora Hunt and Spider Johnson illustrate the variety of artistic alternatives available for the floor.

ted, and sometimes painted. Whatever the method used, they are paintings in fiber, for the floor.

Where the weavers go, can the painters be far behind? They cannot, and they are not.

Painted floorcloths open up the possibility of hanging a painting on the floor. The surface is usually canvas or something equally durable, and the design can be made to suit the taste of the homeowner. This allows personality to triumph over decoration.

The painters that paint surfaces do not discriminate against surfaces that are prostrate. If a wall, or even a ceiling, can be painted to make a personal statement, so can a floor, and the artists are putting their talents to work below our feet as well as at eye level and above. They are giving us floors with geometric patterns, stenciled floors, floors that deceive us into believing that we are walking on marble or exotic woods.

Old wooden floors are rightly treasured for their beauty. Today, contemporary woodworkers can artistically elevate new floors as well. They have taken your basic wooden floor, and inlaid designs into it in ways that make the floor itself a work of art. This floor can stand alone or can serve as an artistic backdrop for a beautiful handwoven rug.

A floor is not a floor is not a floor. A floor is what you make it, and how you look at it. Today's consumers and craft artists are looking at it anew and making a great deal of it.

The work of Hopi weaver Ramona Sakiestewa (top) expresses her involvement with the color and form of the Southwest. Lyn Montagne's rugs (bottom) are ikat dyed, handwoven, and painted.

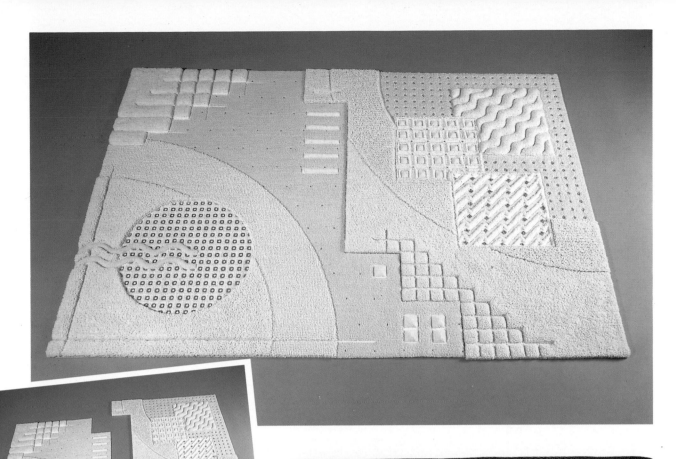

Today's art for the floor is spontaneous, impulsive, energetic, even reckless. Gloria Crouse creates highly textured rugs using variations of hand hooking and sculpting. Her "Creme-de-le-Creme" rug (top) has wool and metal elements and is separable. When the sections are together the rug is 56″ × 79″ and 1½″ deep. Beautifully crafted and elegantly composed, Martha Opdahl's hand-dyed, tufted wool carpets reveal painterly images rich in color. This one (bottom) is 73″ × 99″ and ⅜th of an inch deep.

Form and function meet in a solid, lasting, beautiful way as contemporary fiber artists combine the best of materials and skills to produce floor coverings.

This page: Connie Kindahl specializes in flat woven rugs of wool and linen. This one (top left) is 44" × 79" and is titled "East Mountain." Solveig Nielsen also works in high quality wool yarns on linen warp. She double weaves all of her rugs and each are one of a kind (bottom photos).

Opposite page: Sheree White Sorrells created the 14' × 21' twicewoven rug as a commission for Barbara and Donald Tober. It is entirely hand-dyed in ikat techniques and is a variation of the traditional rag rug.

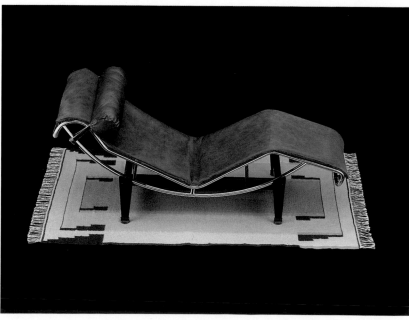

The rugs by Arlyn Ende (top and right) are 100% wool and mohair. Carolyn Bowler's rug with spheres (below) is woven of felted wool strips.

Kathy Cooper specializes in custom designed floorcloths under the label Orchard House Floorcloths. She uses a wide range of imagery in her work including abstract, floral, animals, and vegetables. "Hawaiian Flowers and Stripes" (right) is 5' × 7' and was created for a private residence in Rockville, Maryland.

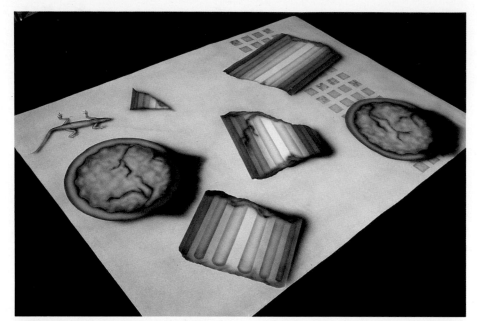

Floorcloths are intended for practical use. These three by Gabriel L. Romeu are acrylic on canvas, which is then varnished many times. The bottom is coated with a non-skid latex rubber. All are 50" × 66" and are painted to be looked down at, so the viewer has an aerial view of the subject.

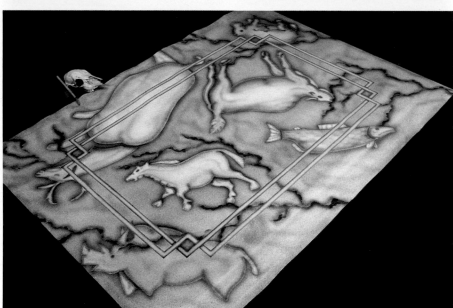

Mary Emery chooses sisal for her hand-painted area rugs because of its ability to hold the delicate details of her artwork. The rugs have finished edges and are latex backed to minimize slipping. Emery Design sisal rugs are pretreated for stain resistance, easy care, and maintenance. The rugs come in a dense yet lightweight needlepoint or a robust doubleweave that projects a more substantial appearance.

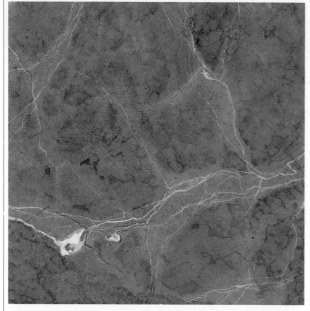

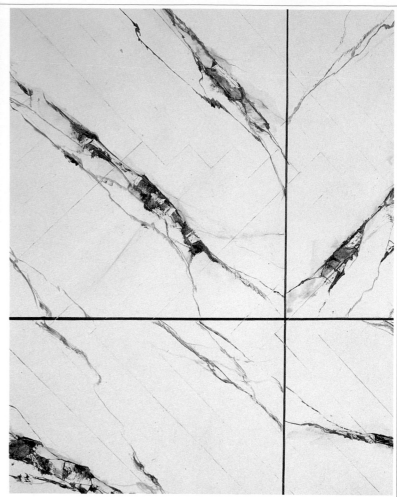

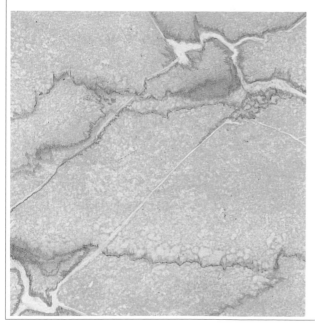

Evergreene Painting Studios offer a wide range of faux finishes for the floor (three left photos). They can turn any basic floor into a work of art—replicating marble, granite, inlaid wood, even fake mosaics. Jim Steere's faux marble floor (right) was painted entirely in oil paint and sealed with high use, non-yellowing methane.

This entry hall with wood marquetry and oak border is 6' × 7' and was designed and installed by Lora Hunt and Spider Johnson. It was commissioned by Walter Germer for his elegant Victorian home in Mason, Texas. The trumpet vine design was inlaid into a parquet of maple, all of which was surrounded by a teak, walnut, and mahogany frame. Special marquetry methods were used to work with the quarter inch thickness of woods used, instead of the usual ¹/₂₈th" thickness. This marquetry was set into the center of the entry, then bordered by red oak flooring.

FOR THE WALL

THE WALLS ARE, AT ONE AND THE SAME TIME, the homeowner's greatest problem and greatest opportunity.

What to do with all that wonderful blank space?

The craft artist has the answer. The craft field has many answers. What once was the exclusive preserve of painters and photographers is now the province of everyone. Art has become democratic, and we are all the better for it.

We can now choose from every medium and from a mixture of media in selecting what will reside on our walls. This new-found freedom to hang a diverse mix of things we love has opened a whole new world of possibilities for the wall.

What we may be witnessing is something that historians will call, in a distant time, the rise of the new masters. The reason is that the craft artist sees the wall not just as an opportunity to display his work and enhance our living spaces, but also as an opportunity to grow both as a technician and an artist. The result is the most exciting new body of work to hit the walls in a very long time.

The weavers have been working on wall pieces for all of recorded history, beginning with the ancient tapes-

Elizabeth MacDonald's pool installation wall piece (top photo) consists of six 3' × 18' panels. Each panel is composed of ceramic tiles approximately 2½" square. The "Amazon Lilies" triptych tapestry by Elaine Ireland (bottom left) is made of wool and cotton with some silk. Alice Van Leunen's paper relief sculpture (bottom middle) is collage and metallic foil. Judy Hubbard used silk habotai, dye, metallic paints, aluminum rods, and metallic threads to create "Where Have All The Flowers Gone?" (bottom right).

A long time dream of a large tapestry version of the Peaceable Kingdom, American style came true for Carol Burland when a client commissioned a work depicting all of the desert animals. After ten months, the 7' × 10' tapestry was completed. It is done in wool, linen, and silk yarns and is entirely hand embroidered.

tries that hang in the great museums of the world. Today all types of fiber artists are creating for the wall, including those where tradition had them start elsewhere—such as quilts that move from the bed to the wall and rugs that rise from the floor to the wall.

Joining the fiber artists in full force are artists working in every other medium imaginable, all of whom are making pieces for the wall in a variety of shapes, sizes, colors, and configurations.

These artists have developed new techniques, have re-thought their media from start to finish, and are creating marvelous things to hang in our homes.

The wall as problem has given way to the wall as opportunity, thanks in large part to the weavers, the glass makers, the ceramists, the papermakers, the metal and woodworkers—the artists who sculpt and paint in every imaginable medium. The new masters.

*This page: "Cybernetics #4: Spectral" is 9′6″ × 2′5″ handwoven of 100%
silk by Anne Lanford Dalton on a computer-interfaced loom. Wendy
Teisberg made the "Stained Glass" (top right) after a visit to see the
Cathedral in St. Paul, Minnesota. The wall piece "Alternate Routes"
(bottom right) was made by Jan Friedman.*

*Opposite page: Wendy Teisberg's "Waterfall" is 5′ × 11′ ¼″ and was
commissioned by Mary and Steve Cherne of Bloomington, Minnesota.*

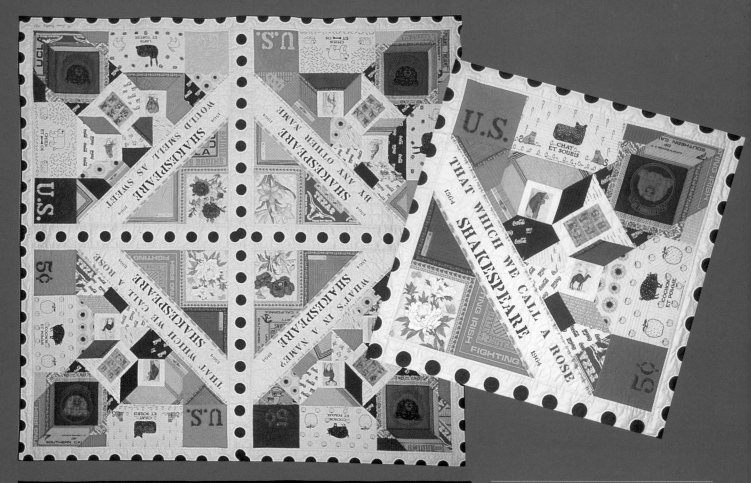

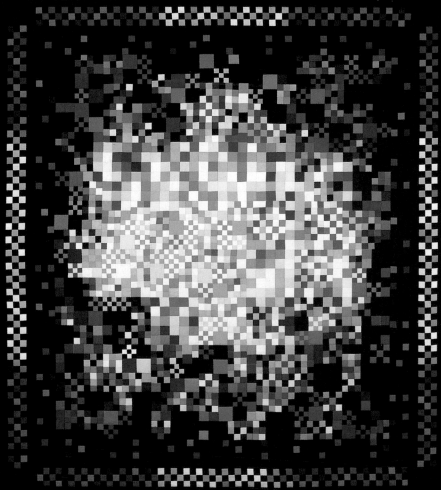

This page: "The Shakespeare Stamp" (top) by Teresa Barkley is 103″ square. Barkley uses a variety of sources for her quilted wall hangings, including scarves, labels, tea towels, and even pages from turn-of-the-century children's books. Susan Webb Lee's quilt (bottom) is titled "Bed-Sized Nebula." It is 78″ × 70″ and is machine quilted of cotton fabrics with cotton polyester batting.

Opposite page: "Interweave 7" (opposite page) by Michael James is 60″ square and is machine-sewn.

"Aqua Flight" is a 4' × 9½' stitched fiber relief by Janet Kuemmerlein which picks up and vivifies the pool's colors. It was commissioned for the residence of Mr. and Mrs. Donald Tranin in Kansas City, Missouri.

Gloria Kosco's handbuilt
fireplace (left) of ceramic tiles
and masonry has cast iron
and tempered glass doors.
"Spikes Galore" (bottom) by
Terri Fletcher is 40" × 80" and
is a two dimensional paper
construction. Fletcher dyed,
scrunched, painted, and
stitched this paper to achieve
the effect she wanted.

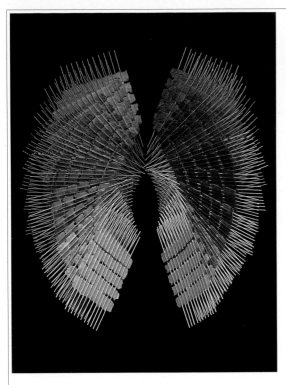

Mary Ann Lomonaco made "Flight" (top left) of handmade abaca paper and painted dowels. It is 42″ × 48″ × 18″ and has been coated for protection and durability. "Flight" works on the principle of gravity inasmuch as it gets its shape from the angle it is hung on the wall. Carol Brown's woven paper construction (top right) is a 39″ × 46″ painting of fiber reactive dyes, gouache, and acrylics on paper. The painting has been torn into strips and reconstructed in a woven form on a loom. The wall sculpture "2.17 Bound Up In Another Illusion" and the sculpture "She Said It Was Best To Keep Illusions In A Box" (bottom), are made of rag paper by Raymond D. Tomasso. Each piece is composed of laminated, hand formed sheets of 100% cotton rag paper. Both pieces are in the collection of Bob Simon of Kansas City, Missouri.

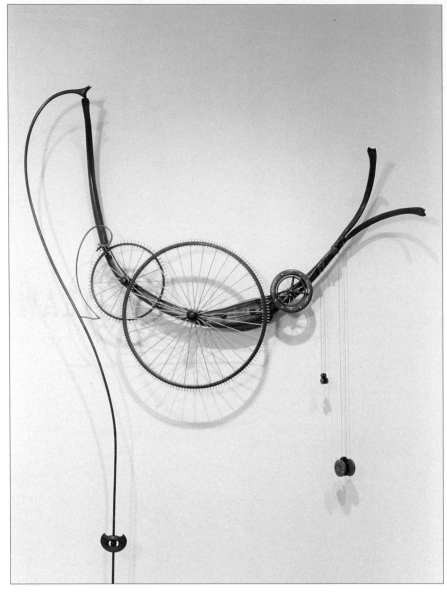

"Clock V-2" is the fifth design in a progression of time sculptures by Larry Hunter. It is 7½' high, 6' long, and wall mounted. Its weight driven running time is 30 hours, which is pendulum regulated. The materials used are walnut, birch, lead, and brass. Ball bearings are used on all wheels and pulleys to ensure low friction, long life, and accuracy. It is accurate to seconds a month. It weighs 15 pounds. The artist devotes a full day to installing the clock and teaching the owner how to use it. By the way, it's 11:43.

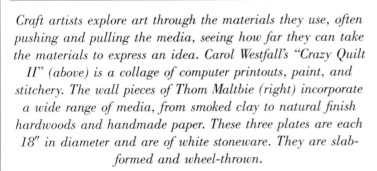

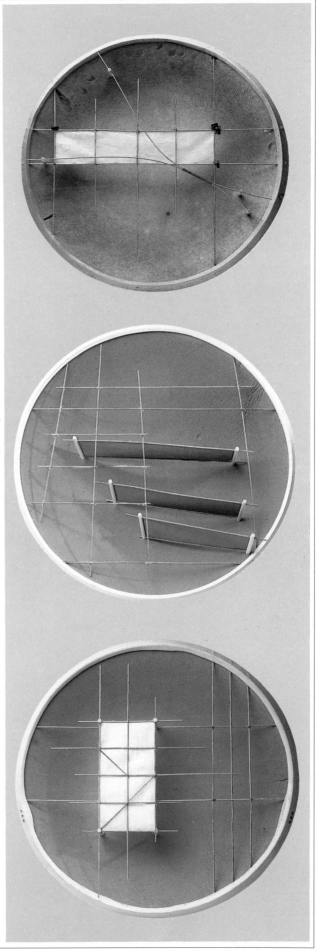

Craft artists explore art through the materials they use, often pushing and pulling the media, seeing how far they can take the materials to express an idea. Carol Westfall's "Crazy Quilt II" (above) is a collage of computer printouts, paint, and stitchery. The wall pieces of Thom Maltbie (right) incorporate a wide range of media, from smoked clay to natural finish hardwoods and handmade paper. These three plates are each 18" in diameter and are of white stoneware. They are slab-formed and wheel-thrown.

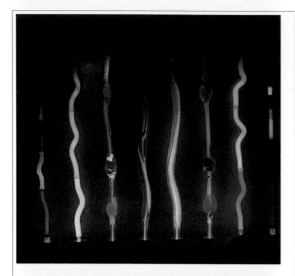

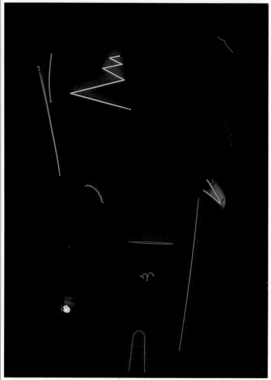

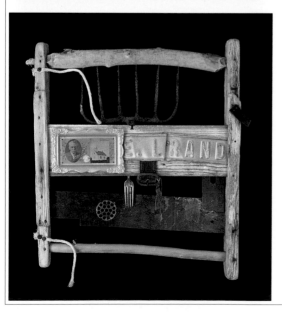

The neon in a mettite wood wall mount (top left) is 2′×2′×6′ and is by Michael Blazek. Jim Harmon created this 10′×10′ "Neon Drawing" (middle left) of hand blown neon tubes to bring liveliness and color to a stairway. J. Fred Woell makes assemblages from objects he finds or from objects of personal significance to clients. His "Requiem at Happy Creek" (bottom left) is 18″×21″×4″ and is designed for wall installation. Carol Adams' "Wallscape XXIX: Palisades" (above) is made of woven forms of various fibers, including metallics, chrome, enamels fired onto copper, and neon.

Susan Starr's 3½' × 5½' wall piece is not overgrown pickup stix; it is made of wood wrapped in handmade paper which bring whimsy and color to the room, and it is titled "Hot Sense."

FURNITURE

NEXT TO THE STRUCTURE ITSELF, FURNITURE is the most fundamental, the most considered, the most used, and the most important part of the home.

To the casual observer, furniture design appears to be a matter of basics. Chairs need legs and backs, tables have to be elevated from the floor, beds should be horizontal, cabinets need shelves at least and probably doors as well. And yet the craft artists who are making furniture continue to surprise us with their originality. The adage "there is nothing new under the sun" is wrong. There is always something new under the artist/furniture maker's sun.

What the craft artist brings to the ABC's of furniture is fresh ideas, inventive techniques, unexpected materials, and a sculptor's eye and view of the world—even of the mundane world of things to sit on, eat around, sleep on, store in. The reasons, then, to look to individual artists for furnishings and furniture are many and wondrous.

Handmade furniture pays homage to the artist's credo that our need for beauty is as basic and as real as our need for food and rest. The artist, no matter if he is creating a painting for the wall or a chair for the table,

This "crafted" room (top) has a table and chest by Judy Kensley McKie, chairs by John Dunnigan with seat covers by Wendy Wahl, Jonathan Bonner's candlesticks, and Janet Prip's vase all resting on a Dunnigan/Wahl carpet. Thomas Stender's whimsical table (bottom left) is of curly maple and curly cherry. The bench (bottom center) of wenge, paint, and leather is by Michael Hurwitz. Peter Dean's grid chair (bottom right) is of mahogany and lacquer with upholstery.

Leon Steele's "Broken Pediment Occasional Chairs" have ten coats of metal lacquer and seven coats of transparent glaze.

been done for centuries. A high tech, handmade chair realizes this apparent—but not real—contradiction somehow.

We are now offered chairs that are funky, fantastic, fundamental, solid, or soul satisfying. What a country full of artists who create furniture can do with four legs, a seat, and a back boggles the mind. They have made what could be mundane a great deal more than that.

And now that ceilings are higher again and the bed-makers have room to put the vertical back into that horizontal and prosaic essential, our sleeping quarters take on new dimensions as well.

Even tables around which we gather for food, cama-raderie, talk, work, family councils are a lot more than legs with a top to lean, write, or eat on.

The flirtation with the lines between art and fantasy and beauty and function is something for the scholars to delineate and describe and debate.

The homes we occupy are the beneficiaries of the movement, whatever name it finally gets in the history books. Our furniture is talking to us, setting moods for our rooms, making our lives brighter and better.

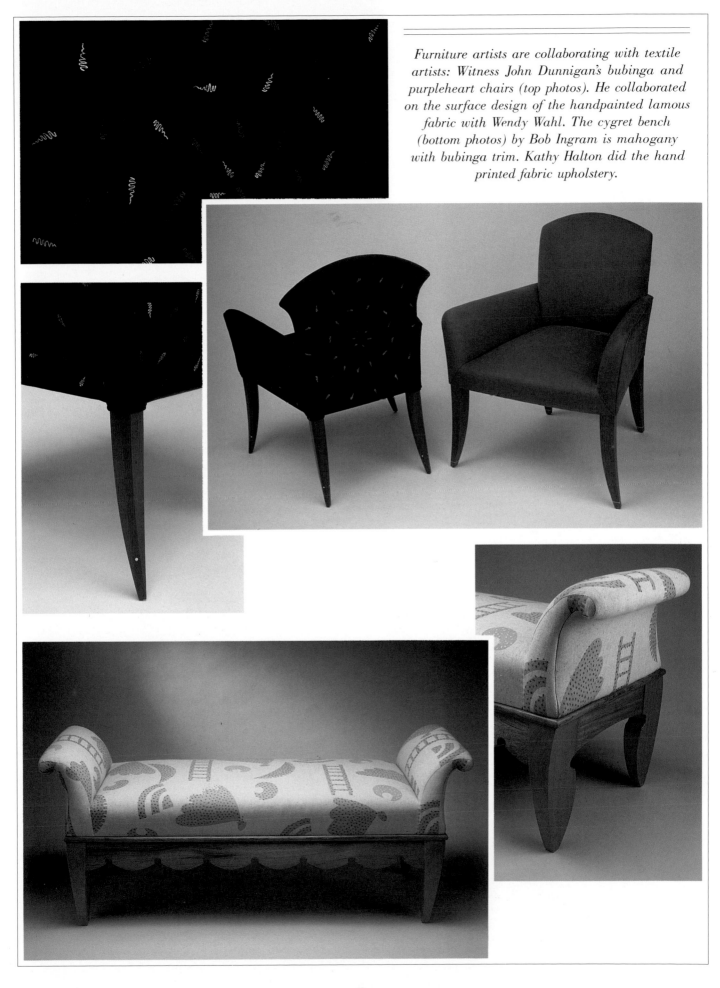

Furniture artists are collaborating with textile artists: Witness John Dunnigan's bubinga and purpleheart chairs (top photos). He collaborated on the surface design of the handpainted lamous fabric with Wendy Wahl. The cygret bench (bottom photos) by Bob Ingram is mahogany with bubinga trim. Kathy Halton did the hand printed fabric upholstery.

Artists find their inspiration anywhere and everywhere. Adirondack furniture and the English garden bench are the thematic sources for the design of this wood slat chair (top) of lacquered pine by Stuart Cohen. A whimsical rendition of a serious classic, Ira A. Keer's high backed easy chair (bottom left) is a celebration of classically inspired elements. Jay Stanger creates abstract, interactive sculpture with his "Bright City Chair" (bottom right).

Whit McLeod's "Folding Wine Barrel Chair" is made out of the staves of old wine barrels and is for sitting (top) or folded flat and putting away (bottom left). He gathers discarded barrels from wineries in the Napa and Sonoma Valleys. Each chair has a unique history in terms of origin of wood, barrel maker, and the vintages which were aged in it. The unique design is not done at the sacrifice of comfort.

This highback chair by Jamie Robertson is made of bleached maple with ebony detailing. The fabric is hand printed, the joinery is traditional, and the finish is lacquer. It was commissioned for Anne and Ron Abramson's collection in Washington, D.C. It is comfortable as well as attractive, an attribute not always present in highback chairs.

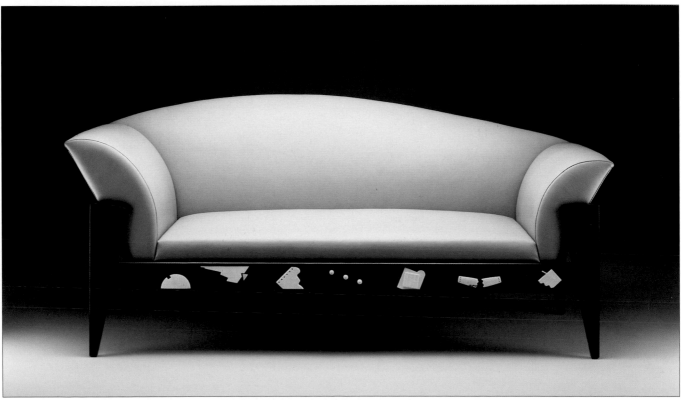

The elegant line and deceptive simplicity distinguish Peter Kramer's bowed stretcher bench (top). Admittedly drawn to early American furniture, Kramer exaggerates this influence in his work. The couch (bottom) is by Rosanne Somerson and is made of ebonized walnut, bleached curly maple, purpleheart, and leather.

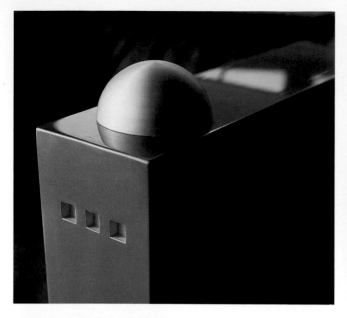

David Woolf's space age hanging table (bottom left) is a perfect complement to his high tech rocking chair (top photos). The aluminum and stainless steel chair (above) is by Vered Blatman.

John Randolph and Bruce Tomb created this granite cooktop of everything imaginable: a steel fire extinguisher tank, camp stove parts, a granite cooktop, cast plastic knobs, pulled together with stainless steel tierods and aluminum paint.

The "Katsura" bed, designed by Anthony Di Guiseppe, with its storage drawers and side tables, has a pearwood body with ebonized ash table and shelf tops; inlays and headboard frame are purpleheart wood; grey leather headboard.

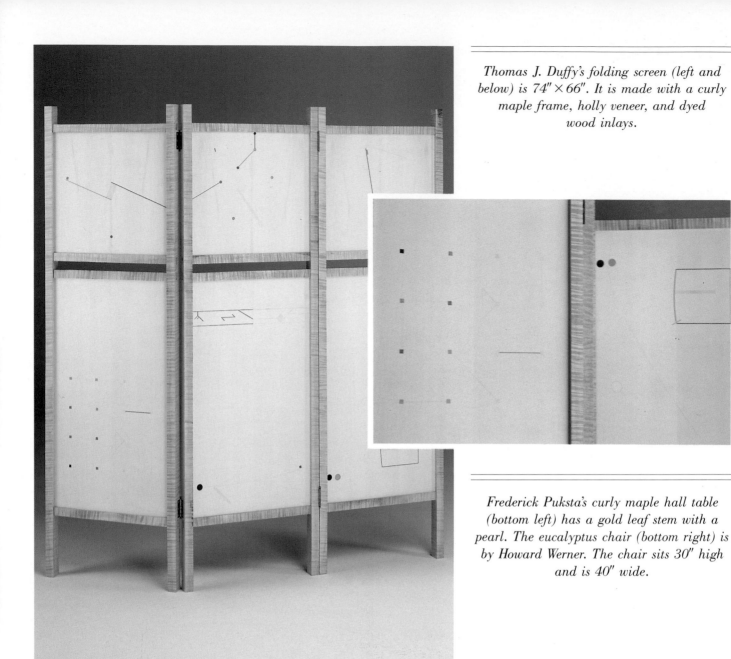

Thomas J. Duffy's folding screen (left and below) is 74″ × 66″. It is made with a curly maple frame, holly veneer, and dyed wood inlays.

Frederick Puksta's curly maple hall table (bottom left) has a gold leaf stem with a pearl. The eucalyptus chair (bottom right) is by Howard Werner. The chair sits 30″ high and is 40″ wide.

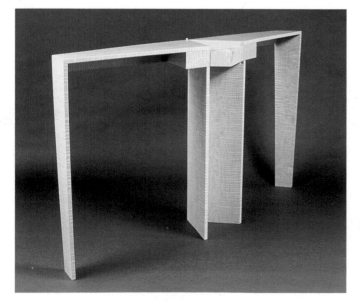

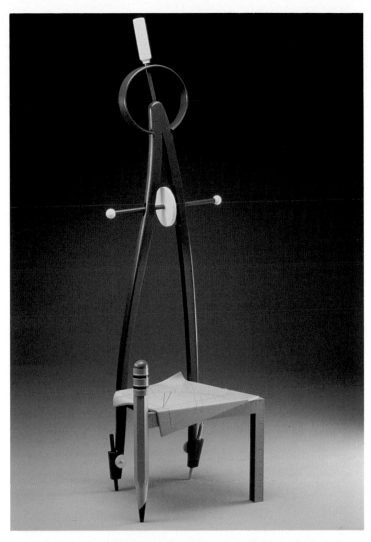

Alphonse Mattia did this imaginative "Architect's Valet" (top left). C.H. Becksvoort's music stand is of laminated black cherry and his bowback chair (bottom left) is of black cherry and ash. Thomas J. Beck made his bookstand (below) of walnut with birdseye maple trim. It is lighted by a 40 watt bulb.

John Hein prefers to use woods with suggestive patterns, such as in his cabinet (top photos). It is made of Queensland walnut with ebony door pulls, and is 65½" high, 41½" wide, and 11" deep. Janice Smith's imaginatively designed "Harlequin" chest of drawers is made of rift sawn red oak and mahogany with mirror inserts.

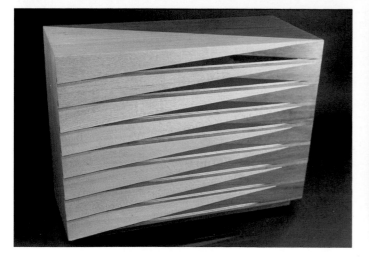

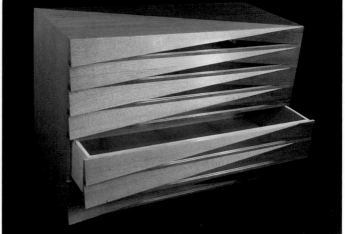

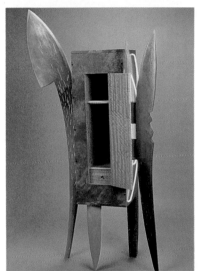
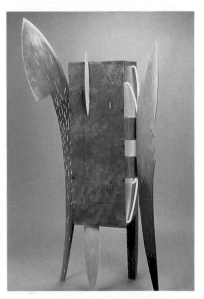

The marriage of function and fine art is not always a harmonious one, but the two pieces on this page bring it off winningly. The liquor cabinet is by Jay Stanger (left), and the brandy cabinet (right) is Wendy Maruyama's.

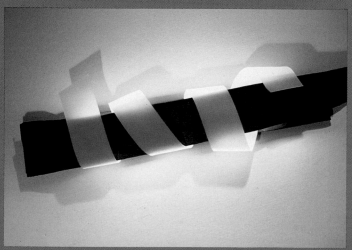

LIGHTING

WHEN THOMAS EDISON INVENTED THE ELEC-tric light bulb over 100 years ago, he created a design opportunity for the home. Unfortunately it is a design opportunity that was largely ignored until recently.

Tiffany, of course, brought the art of craft to lighting, combining glass and metal to create lamps that literally made rooms glow. Since his time we've been stuck with mostly boring lamps and big shades until the contemporary European designers introduced the high tech, high style halogen lamps.

Now there is another revolution in lighting— American craft artists are moving strongly into illumination design. They are creating lighting that stands on the floor, sits on the table, hangs from the ceiling, leans against the wall, is attached to the wall, and everything in between.

They are working with every imaginable material, and the range of their designs starts at bare bones high tech and moves steadily into sculptural and often beyond that to the consciously ornate. Folksy, primitive, futuristic, all that and more as they create lamps and lighting for the home and for the grounds outside the home as well.

What they are producing could be appropriately called jewelry for the home, which it is. But it is more

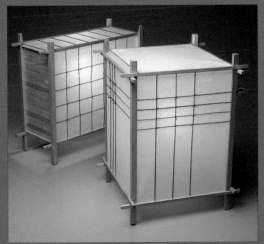

The large and the small of it in lighting are embodied in Lyn Hovey's dream kitchen with the inverted bent stained glass ceiling lamp (top) complemented by a wall mounted light by Denise Leone (bottom left), an archetype table lamp by Stuber/Stone (bottom center), and Thomas Maltbie's two lanterns (bottom right).

than that. Objects that are made to light may be art, but lighting is a science as well. If a lighting design is to work, the craft artist must be part engineer and deal with the subtle, elusive phenomenon of mood alteration.

Lighting is a whole lot more than simply illuminating what is dark. When you enter a room that is well lit, you take on the mood that the artist/ designer has created. You may be cheered, you may feel romantic, you may be soothed. The reason is that lighting is a truly magical phenomenon.

In the craft of lighting, as in all crafts but more strongly here than elsewhere, the best work combines utility and beauty. If the combination is right, it truly enlivens the spirit and elevates the mood.

Chandeliers range from C.H. Becksvoort's in simple wood for candles (left) to David Ponsler's forged steel (right).

"Murnau, 1909" (above) is by Joe Porcelli. It stands 27½" high, is 20" in diameter and is made of mold-formed leaded glass, copper, brass, and steel. It is a contemporary manipulation of leaded glass lampmaking techniques developed by Tiffany. Todd Noe's floor lamps (top right) are 60" high, made of handblown glass with a painted brass shaft on a cast concrete base. Sidney Hutter's lamps (bottom photos) are cut, ground, laminated plate glass and come in all sizes and vary in scale from tabletop to floor and wall constructions. Hutter considers his lamps "miniature buildings" because of their architectural design.

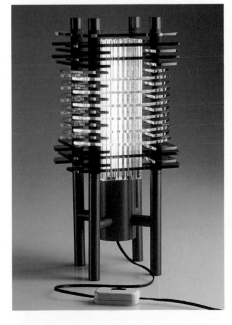

Curtis and Suzan Benzle's porcelain light columns are framed in aluminum with a plexiglas core. They capture light and shadow and are striking in closed areas without natural light.

Keith Crowder's "Shaman Lights" of poplar, purpleheart, ash, waxed jute, and string lean against the wall and can easily be moved around the room.

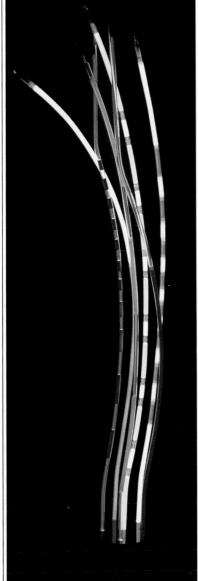

Al Blankschien's neon sculpture entitled "Candy Factory" (left) is 7 feet tall. David Baird's wall-floor lights (right photos) are 6 feet tall. The fitting is made of oxidized steel and features a sculptured shape silhouetted against a pool of light radiating in oblique directions.

Isaac Maxwell's bracket light (top left) is brass with tin-lead flood over the un-punched areas; his fan shaped bracket light (bottom left) is copper and brass with a verde finish. Ruth Siegel created the glass door and matching sconces (right) for the New York apartment of Mr. and Mrs. David Gethen. Siegel carefully selects the colors and textures of the glass to create pleasant variations of light.

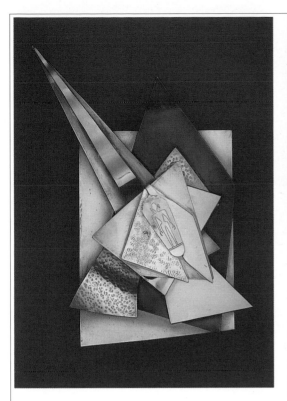

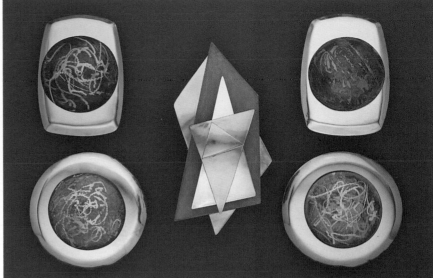

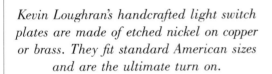

Kevin Loughran's handcrafted light switch plates are made of etched nickel on copper or brass. They fit standard American sizes and are the ultimate turn on.

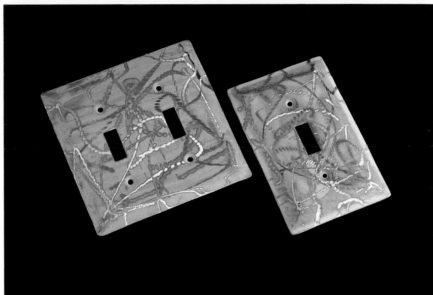

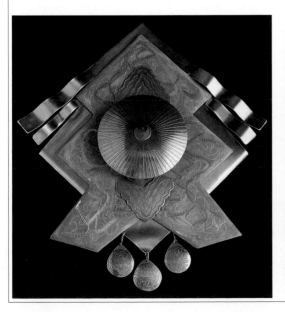

This page: Ray King created this exterior sculptural frieze of bronze elements, patinated in a range of colors with optical glass fins, prisms, and lenses. Opposite page: The landscape lights by Bradley Cross are made of sandcast bronze and brass tubing with copper leaves. They stand about 30" above the ground.

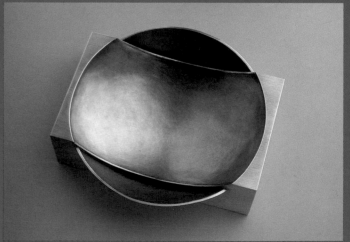

OBJECTS

WE ARE WHAT WE EAT . . . PHYSICALLY. WE are what we read . . . intellectually. And we are what we collect . . . aesthetically. The urge to gather and display is universal, and today's craft artists are providing us with a cornucopia of wonderful objects—from the purely utilitarian to the emphatically decorative—that give us more and more ways to satisfy that universal urge.

The essence of craft is the celebration of the object. Beautiful, original objects that fulfill functional requirements are the root and heart of this varied field. These objects can be simple and plain or elaborately ornate, but traditionally they perform tasks.

Craft has always implied function; what craft artists are helping us discover is that while the adjectives functional and utilitarian are close, they are not synonymous. The function does not have to be utilitarian. The function may simply be to be beautiful, to decorate, to enhance a place or a space, to evoke an emotional response.

Collecting breathes life into art, and whatever an object's function is in this land somewhere between utilitarian and decorative, these are very much our things, and they help define us. A home that is filled

Mixed media artist Wolf did this eclectic wall installation in the Virginia Tomlinson home (top) using clocks, photo frames, and mirrors. Kira Louscher's non-functional flatware pieces (bottom left) are 7" long and are of copper, bronze, and silver. Hyewon Lee's vessel (bottom center) is of pewter. Sarah Belcher made her box with moving wheels (bottom right) of brass, feathers, and semi-precious stones.

Joan Irving's perfume bottles of sculptured glass
please more than the sense of smell. These are of
¾″ glass that has been slumped, sand-blasted,
and painted.

with objects of every kind, shape, size, color, and material reveals volumes about the occupants of the home.

We step into each other's homes and share these objects—full of humor, elegance, maybe even a touch of kitsch. Not only the objects but the aesthetic styles can range from the highly embellished country and folk to austere and classic traditional to high tech and hard edged minimalism. All styles can live together, complementing one another and reflecting our own personalities.

We are also learning that our beloved objects belong everywhere in our homes. The things we collect do not have to be on pedestals or under spotlights. Refusing to accept anybody else's idea of "where things go," we put our prizes in niches, on busy shelves, in rooms as utilitarian as the laundry or the bath. And then we look at them and use them, or just look at them—and truly live with the things we love.

A ceramic tea cup can make you feel good when you drink from it; the texture, shape, and color is a pleasure to hold and to behold.

The mysterious wooden box with hidden compartments holds secrets as well as possessions.

The sculptured glass bowl that sits on the mantel looks different from every angle, in every light, at every time of day, and does things to the psyche as well as to the room and the home it graces.

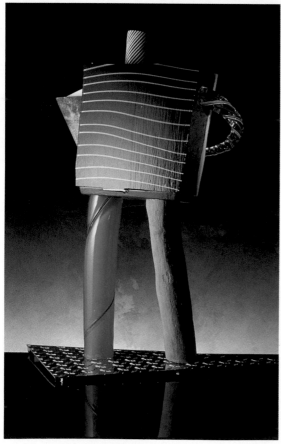

Steve Maslach's dichroic bowl (top), the "Non Skid T-Pot" by Kerry Feldman (bottom left), and Sidney Hutter's stacked glass vase (bottom right) are exceptional examples of collectible glass objects.

Robert Shenfield's large ceramic vessel is wheel-thrown. The dry-matte surface is composed of slips over a stoneware clay body, with underglazes then airbrushed onto the surface.

Kathleen Dustin made this 25″ high ceramic wall sculpture (top photos) titled "The First Apartment." Robert McCandless' "Lighted Bookends" (bottom photos) are made of marble, sandblasted glass, and acrylic.

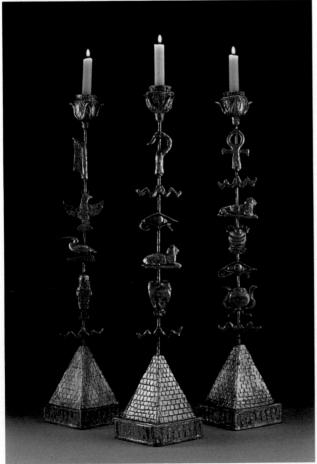

Albert Paley sculpted this epic fireplace structure (top) from forged and fabricated steel. It is 7' high and 6½' wide. The three soaring candlesticks (bottom) are by Thomas McCanna. Each one is individually handcrafted using low-fire clay combined with welded iron.

The sculptural basketry of Nancy Moore Bess is unusual and imaginative. Utilizing traditional techniques of basket weaving, fencing, and thatching, Bess combines raffia and chamois with accent elements to create her basket forms.

The creative use of unusual, unthinkable materials distinguish the decorative objects on this page: There are Karyl Sisson's "Container VII" (top photos) made of stained wood clothespins and wire, Cynthia Porter's "Fiber House" (bottom left), and Howard Werner's "Sycamore Spiral" (bottom right).

Many artists use their talents to create drama and surprise. Po Shun Leong's "Landscape" box for precious objects (top photos) contains 18 disappearing pivoting drawers surrounding a miniature landscape of architectural elements. "Dream Box: Negative Double Positive" (bottom) is Dina Angel-Wing's mixed media sculpture.

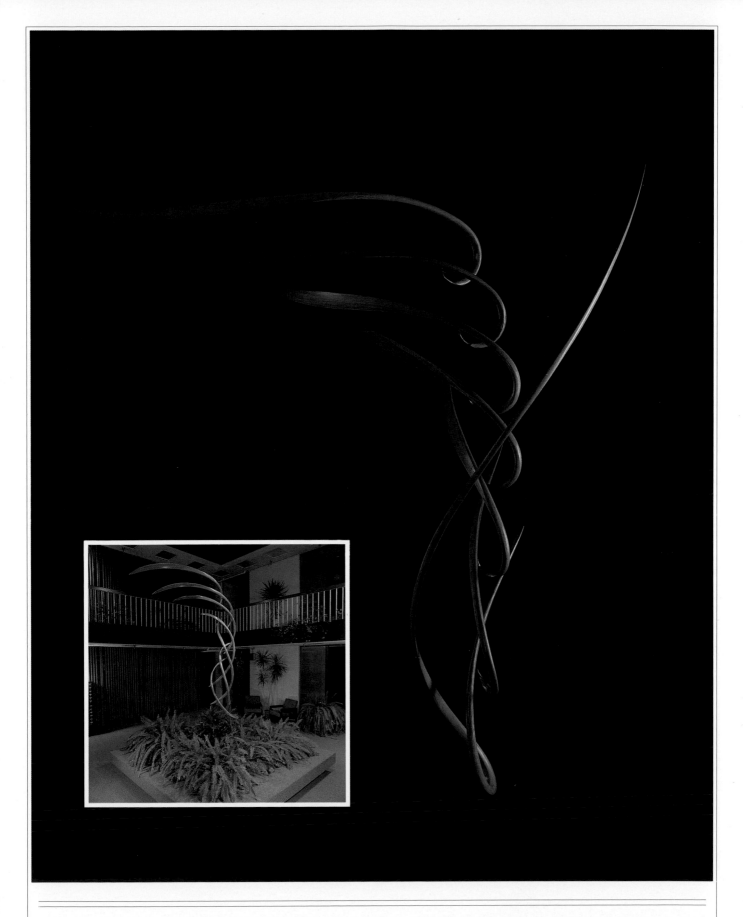

Jonathan Clowes created "Haiku for Nancy" for John and Nancy Lightbody. It hangs in the open stairwell of their contemporary home in Falmouth, Maine where it is visible from all the spaces of the house. The sculpture, of laminated ash veneers, dances in the drafts that are always moving in the stairway.

Among the wonderful objects being created by contemporary metal artists are Christopher Ellison's brass and steel vessel (top), Shari Mendelson's copper and patina vessel (bottom left), and Janet Prip's 13″ × 4½″ × 1½″ pewter head vases (bottom right).

Keith Jellum calls his sculpture the "Welsh Windship" to set it apart from the traditional concept of weathervanes. It is 37" high, 94" wide, and 17" deep. This windship is made of fabricated bronze, and it soars and turns magnificently with the wind.

FOR THE BATH

SURELY THE MOST UNLIKELY SHOWCASE FOR the work of craft artists in the home is that paragon of practical, antiseptic efficiency, the bath. But take another look. In the bathroom we have wood cabinetry, ceramic tiles, metal fixtures, stained glass windows, one-of-a-kind lighting, and surfaces just asking to be painted. This room, contrary to all expectations, provides us with many opportunities to be artistically creative.

No other room reflects lifestyle changes more than the bathroom. It has become a place where we pamper ourselves. The luxurious bath with the sauna and the whirlpool and the exercise corner and the rocking chair for recovering from the sauna, the whirlpool, and the exercise corner is probably the preserve of a minority; the elegant bath, however, is definitely here to stay.

But elegant is only one way to go. There is the loud and funky bathroom or the romantically indulgent room. All of this and more can be achieved with the talented help of today's craft artists.

What craft artists can do with the tiles on the walls, with painting the surfaces of the walls themselves, is immediately obvious and desirable.

And the opportunity for glass windows and skylights

The ordinary becomes the extraordinary with a little imagination and a talented artist. Marcy Pesner's tiles (top) are of walnut with colored ash for the mosaic inlay set on an oak baseboard. The handmade sinks and countertop (bottom left) by Kathryn Allen are made of glazed stoneware. The ceramic tile relief (bottom center) is by Totten/Harnden. Judith Robertson's mosaic sink (bottom right) shows what you can do with a fundamental fixture if you put your mind to it.

David Wright made these porcelain tiles around a bathtub of three different thicknesses, providing the look of a mosaic.

that do more than simply let light in, which is a relatively new phenomenon in what used to be a tomblike space, is just now being explored and expanded.

A sink is a mosaic canvas, a floor is another. Even bathtubs can be transformed through the artfulness of the woodworker.

The small half bath in what might have been a closet is a chance for the artist to enliven, enlighten and even delude us into believing the space is bigger than it really is.

Not every bath is a work of art, but every bath can be, and more and more homeowners are insisting on it.

Jamie Fine's 4¼″ square ceramic tiles were designed to surround the clawfoot tub in Jacqueline Wright's Ann Arbor, Michigan home (top). The tiles were airbrushed over resist with low-fire glaze. Gordon Bryan's relief ceramic tiles (bottom) are hand-pressed, hand-cut, and custom glazed. These tiles in a bathroom wall installation are 12″ tall.

This page: The Egyptian motif tiles in this bathroom (top photos) are by Deborah Hecht. The entire 8' × 6½' bathroom (left) was designed by Ted Galeza to have a feeling of openness both inside and with the outside. The matching blues of the walls, sky, floor, sink and towels, the ceramic tile becoming glass block along one entire wall, and the clear glass utility wall which acts to separate the shower area are all tied together with a checkerboard taxi stripe.

Opposite page: The floor, ceiling, and walls are of handmade ceramic tile relief in this "Underwater Bath" designed and fabricated by Chuck Totten and Cherie Harnden. This enormous commission consists of 270 sq. ft. of tile.

Judith Robertson's fully functional mosaic-tiled porcelain pedestal sink is shown in all its colorful glory here in the bathroom that it brings gloriously to life.

Laney Oxman created this life size
environment of ladies, dogs, fish,
flowers, and victorian furniture that
has become the bathroom in the
Bethesda, Maryland home of Fred
and Starr Ezra. Oxman's materials
are white earthenware clay
and mirrors.

119

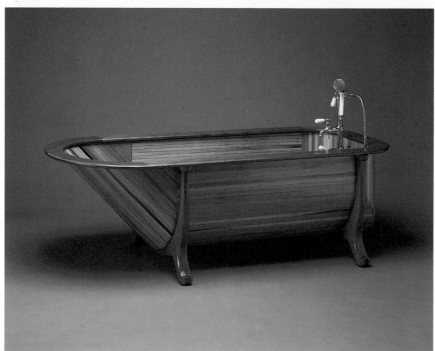

Suzanne VanGalder specializes in custom designed contemporary stained glass like this 8' × 4' window for the bathroom (top). Jo and Jon Birdsey use aerospace construction techniques and finishes in combination with rare woods and metals to create this elegant tub (left).

Glass artist Lyn Hovey and woodworker Jamie Robertson created this fantasy environment from a Hovey design. The nymph lolling in the lily pond is actually a self-illuminating mirror, part reflective glass, part hand-painted translucent glass. To contain the image Robertson created mahogany bas-relief leaves and a swirling sink pedestal.

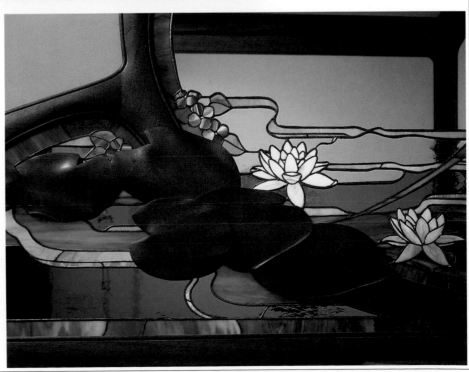

The abstraction of rocks and water for this private bath by Lyn Hovey integrates design and function. The stained glass provides the bath area with privacy, while the special inside mounting of the glass preserves the thermal-glazed and ventilation features of the windows.

ARCHITECTURAL GLASS

GLASS AND THE ARTISTS WHO WORK WITH glass are in full flower, and they are turning their attention and talents to the architecture of homes. As a result, there is a lot more for the glass in our windows and in our doors to do than show us what is outside or to show outsiders what is inside.

Artists are etching the glass for these apertures, beveling it, sandblasting it, slump-casting it, fusing it, and making special stained glass pieces for certain openings. They have opened up a whole, intriguing spectrum of glass design to tantalize us. Glass catches the imagination; it floats like the air, sparkles like fire, yet is cool to the touch like water.

And this magical medium is moving to the inside of the house as well as being used in structural ways. The work of glass artists is being used to add a spot of color on the wall, to divide a room, as a glass brick facade for the fireplace.

Glass adds so much to any environment, and now that craftsmen have figured out ways to show and con-

The "Morning-Glories" window by Lyn Hovey (top photo) brings color and light to the room, as does Jean Myer's 185 sq. ft. of entry wall windows (bottom left). Larry Zgoda's circlehead window (bottom center) and the stair landing windows by Pegasus Studio (bottom right) allow a view with privacy.

127

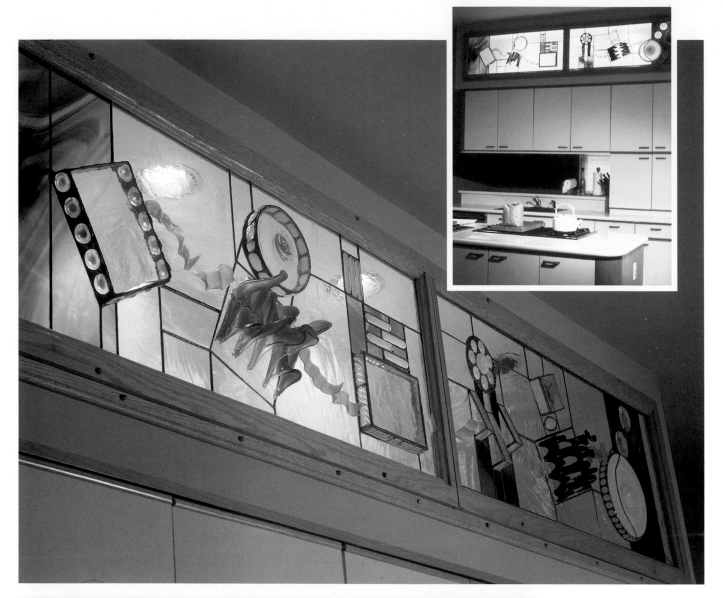

Saara Gallin's "Dancers"
(top photos), backlit glass
above the kitchen cabinets,
are of antique stained glass
and copper foil technique,
slumped glass, and Tiffany
jewels. Gallin's work is
almost always in relief,
where she can offer her
client a multitude of three
dimensional forms. Lenn
Neff's two windows (left)
are a contemporary
interpretation of St.
Petersburg, Florida's
downtown activities—the
beach, the parades, and
outdoor festivals.

ceal through glass simultaneously, they are moving beyond transparency to bring dead corners, airshafts for Heaven's sake, to glittering life. They have figured out new ways to harness our precious light—glass allows the natural light in and creates openness, while maintaining privacy at the same time.

The technological revolution in glass is paralleling the artistic one. Glass artists have learned as much about the possibilities of glass in the last 20 years as in the previous 200. New kinds of glass and other materials are being wedded to new processes, and the result is that an old medium is being transformed into an exciting new medium. The glass artist can now sculpt with the same kind of facility as the wood or stone or clay artist can.

The artists working in this field have gone so far so fast with new techniques and uses for glass that the general public is a step and a half behind the artistic and technological possibilities. But they are catching up fast, and because they are the world is a better looking place, whether you are looking out at it, in on it, or at what is inside.

Lenn Neff's kitchen window, cabinet doors and sconces obscure the contents of the cabinets and the house next door yet admit all of the light from the outside. The design is basically a "temple to the preparation of sustenance."

© 1989 Bruce Fritz

© 1989 Bruce Fritz

Larry Zgoda was faced with several architectural considerations in designing these three stained glass panels. The windows are transoms, which is classic in Victorian houses where stained glass would have been included in the original design. The designs chosen offer a hint of the early modernism of the house and create a compositional tension.

130

The 6' "Octagon Window" by Narcissus
Quagliata was fabricated of custom blown
stained glass for a residence in Malibu,
California.

"Dining Room Window" was created for the breakfast room of the Person residence in Denver, Colorado by J. Gorsuch Collins. It is beveled and sandblasted using antique and hand-rolled glass. Collins' subtle color combinations complement the room and make every breakfast a feast for the eyes at the very least.

This page: The 9′ × 12′ custom blown and sandblasted glass with unique bevels was designed by Narcissus Quagliata to separate the dining from the living room in a Manhattan penthouse. The hand blown roundel (left) is a Quagliata signature.

Opposite page: "Gala Reflections," a screen by Maya Radoczy, is 11′ high and 10′ wide and rises free-standing out of a granite floor. It is composed of leaded, hand blown glass and fused elements created by the artist. The screen fulfills its role of dividing the two rooms while allowing light into the interior spaces.

This page: Paul Marioni is a pioneer in the use of architectural cast glass. He created the 6' × 4' "Solar Fireplace" with the assistance of Ann Troutner. It is cast of clear glass; the mirrored back reflects the light evenly to appear as a window.

Opposite page: Nancy Gong's dimensionally carved glass art panels set in light wells add a decorative accent while opening the space up and letting light in. The panels add simple elegance to this residence in Rochester, New York.

Thomas Holzer fashioned architectural custom art glass using genuine mouth-blown antique glasses with cast glass jewels for the windows, doors, and panels that enliven and enhance these private residences.

Wilfred Bissonnette's 9' × 10' front entry was created for a client in Ridgefield, Connecticut. The interior decor had an oriental motif which Bissonnette reflected in his windows. They are bronze laminated thermal pane set in a white oak frame.

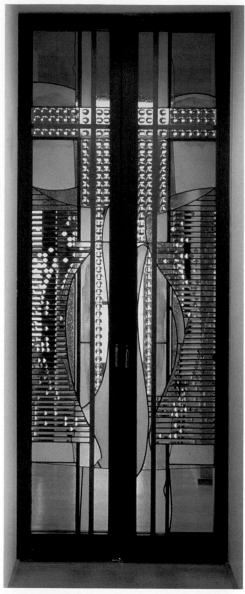

This page: David Wilson's leaded glass door and side windows (left center and top center) are for a Florida residence. The doors to a master bedroom suite (top right) are by Ken vonRoenn, who used beveled glass to fracture the view and take advantage of available light. The main entry doors for a home in Anchorage, Kentucky (bottom) are designed by vonRoenn to obscure the view and provide privacy as well as to elevate the presence of the entry.

Opposite page: The entry to the Rigney home in Woodland Hills, California is by Jane Skeeter. It consists of two lower sidelites, two upper sidelites, and a center transom. All are leaded, beveled, and various textures of clear glass and incorporate antique crystal jewels of unusual shapes and sizes.

THE TAILOR-MADE ENVIRONMENT

THE ULTIMATE LUXURY IS HAVING SOMETHING tailor-made for you. A shirt is nice. A suit is better. A house is best. Bits and pieces of a house are very good too. An environment. A hand-made, tailor-made environment just for you, your family and your friends.

When you commission an artist to design and make something especially for your home, you are essentially creating your own tailor-made environment. You are adding a personal signature.

Commissioning means that you become a part of the design process, a member of the design team as it were. The consumer of mass produced goods, on the other hand, simply chooses among the options offered. This should not be taken to mean that the choices are limited. They are myriad. The industrial revolution may have had its faults; limited choices was not one of them. But with all of our immense industrial capabilities, only artists have the ability to create things and places which reflect one's individual style and uniqueness.

The art of tailor-making is encapsulated on these pages: there's Juan and Patricia Navarrete's bedroom fireplace (top) of gypsum plaster, Scott Goewey's wall (bottom left) of stoneware clay, a marquetry door panel (bottom center) by Rick Wrigley, and "Palampore" by Zoe Lancaster (bottom right), hand screen printed on linen and cotton fabric.

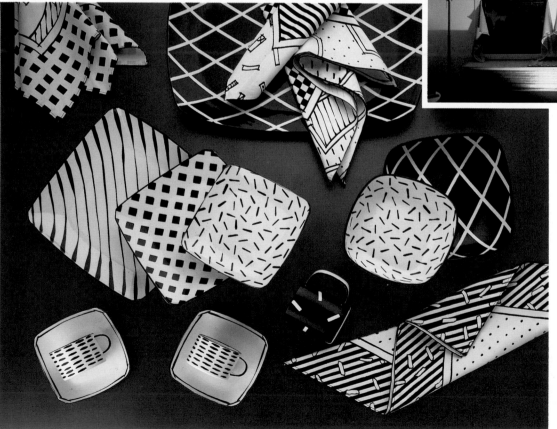

Karen Cullen made the elegantly simple "Zipper Curtains" (top photos). The plates and cloths for the table (left) are by Dorothy Hafner.

To choose among manufactured objects is one thing. To be involved in the design of what you live with is quite another thing altogether. Active participation in the creation of your own environment is what commissioning is all about.

Commissioning an artist to make something original for you implies a kind of singularity. There is great joy and satisfaction to be found in the dinner service that matches your eclectic lifestyle, or the fireplace that fits the unusual requirements of your living room, or the specially designed curtains that let the light in, give you a visual treat, and block an otherwise ugly view.

The world is full of artists who are making everything imaginable. They are adept at finding beautiful and functional solutions to design problems.

Most artists enjoy collaborating with their clients. They enjoy the challenges presented by unique situations. Oftentimes they say that the best solutions are discovered in the commission process, not designed at the outset. There are no formulas here, and that alone appeals to the artistic species.

The process starts with a design problem or opportunity. Do you have

This ceramic tile fireplace and hearth is by Steven Goldner of Starbuck Goldner Studios. The tiles are of pressed white stoneware, glazed, and are ¾" relief. They also meet strict standards for strength and heat resistance.

an unappetizing view, a space that is not adequate for the proposed use, a case of the blahs? Do you want to enhance and beautify a relatively problem-free space? Whatever. The tailor-made solution starts with the selection of an artist who is likely to produce an answer that fits your style, taste, and budget. Once the artist is chosen and agrees to the commission, design begins.

While the best commissions are often true collaborations between artist and client, it is up to you to decide just how actively you will participate in the design of what you seek. Collaboration takes many forms. In most cases the commissioner will present the situation and let the artist create an appropriate response.

What the artist brings to you is experience and the particularly rare skill of designing for the living environment. This goes beyond creating something visually striking; it extends to making sure the work is exacting in its quality and that it meets your articulated requirements. You, the client, get the benefit of the craft artist's professional knowledge of materials, scale, shapes, and the techniques of problem solving that are such important pieces of solving the tailor-making puzzle.

Opposite page: Artist/ blacksmith Jack Brubaker designed and forged strap hinges and thumb latch out of steel for this door. Ronald Schuster did the stained glass panels.

147

This page: Lyn Hovey designed this swan and jewel stairway window and the custom nouveau sash with the help of Jamie Robertson who did the woodwork.

Opposite page: Roger Reid made the corner cabinet for Peter and Wendy Pearson of Canton, Connecticut; it is all mahogany with heavily figured panels.

Anything can be commissioned. While the word "commission" brings to mind something grandiose like a public monument or an oil portrait, the fact is that commissioning is something anyone, and everyone can do. And a commission can be for something as small as a door latch, or a door, or a railing for the steps that lead to the door. If this is new to you, the craft artist can help take the apprehension out. The artist is there to make your dreams, large or small, come true.

If you have a window that overlooks an air shaft, the problem is an obvious one: to make an eyesore into a place that admits light and pleases the eye. The solution might be a window of stained glass, etched glass, painted glass or even a creative manipulation of industrial glass with modest decorative elements. It can be an elaborate or a simple solution, depending on the room, the artist, and you.

Or perhaps you have a set of china that deserves to be seen between those occasions when it is in use, and you need something that holds and displays, adorns rather than clutters the room, and fits the space available to the dual tasks. You can go to the furniture showrooms or the antique stores and, perhaps, find what you seek, but you can also, often for the same kind of

This elegant bar by Peter Dean uses a multitude of beautiful woods: Indian rosewood, purpleheart, pearwood, and curly birdseye maple. The counter is marble, and the fixtures are brass.

money, commission a woodworker to tailor something for the room and the contents.

It isn't always that simple. A commission to design and build a bar/liquor cabinet which is a prominent part of a large room, for example, is a lot more complicated. There are likely to be long discussions about how the room is to be used, what lifestyles are being accommodated here. The look

of the room. The eye of the user. Something as subliminal as how the user reacts to which colors is likely to be probed by the artist in search of a design solution that pleases not just the eye but the emotional needs of the user as well. There will be drawings made and rejected and altered and selected. The design part of the process can be as lengthy as the crafting itself.

When the process is over, the design made, the designed work crafted, it should fit, as if it had been, what? Tailor-made, of course, which it will have been. But there is more gratification than simply having personalized an environment, there is the gratification of having collaborated, participated in the creation of this space and of having something uniquely yours.

There are many options available for tailoring living spaces to reflect our individual personal aesthetics. Considerable satisfaction comes from working with an artist who can join your ideas to his and turn these combined ideas into a finished product. Even greater satisfaction comes from living with the end result—a tailor-made environment.

This 16' high fireplace by Elizabeth MacDonald is composed of 1500 tiles and is colored with a blue slip and powdered Mason stains pressed into wet clay. Each tile contains its own world as it creates another.

Chris Hughes' steel and brass balcony railing (top) gives a feeling of weightlessness to the stair. Ellen Kochansky's pieced quilt (bottom left) is appropriately titled "Dreams Landscape," which it suborns. And is there a more appropriate finale to this paean to personalization than Carolyn and Vincent Carleton's personal signature on their hand Jacquard woven carpet?

This door by Wayne Brungard opens up a world of creative possibilities.

AMERICAN CRAFTS AWARDS

OVER FIVE THOUSAND CRAFT ARTISTS HAVE ENTERED THE ANNUAL American Crafts Awards inaugurated by Kraus Sikes Inc. in 1987. This major national competition, the largest in the crafts field, recognizes the exciting new products being created for the home. The awards honor the best new designs married with fine craftsmanship in a number of categories.

The categories have changed over the years, as have the winners in the categories. What has not changed is the quality of the work being submitted for judging. The competition started with a plethora of excellence for the sorely beset judges to choose among, and, if anything, the work has gotten better and the choices more difficult.

The winners of the American Crafts Awards in the first two years of its existence are listed on the next few pages. In addition, most of the winners are featured in this book so the reader can see for himself what is being achieved by contemporary craft artists.

Work that is made of traditional materials using traditional techniques is displayed alongside pieces made in unexpected ways with innovative materials.

It is an eclectic business, this business of crafts.

Work that is created in the hills of a sparsely settled western state wins plaudits as does that produced in artists' studios in major cities in this country.

It is a geographically diverse business, this business of crafts.

Work done by men and women who have devoted their working lives to honing their skills is honored alongside the work of relative newcomers to the field who bring fresh insights and ideas to art forms that have been around for centuries.

It is an ageless business, or an age-irrelevant business, this business of crafts.

The hills are alive with craft artists doing amazing work, and so are the streets, and the artistic colonies in rural and urban America.

What's more, we are discovering them in all of these places, celebrating their talents, and bringing their work into our homes. As it should be.

GRAND PRIZE WINNERS

Merit Award Winners

FUNCTIONAL DECORATIVE OBJECTS:

David Baird	La Jolla, CA	93
Boris Bally	N. Quincy, MA	36
Susan M. Bankert	Detroit, MI	33
Sarah D. Belcher	Brooklyn, NY	99
Butter + Toast	Providence, RI	33
Mardi-Jo Cohen	Philadelphia, PA	36
Keith Crowder	Providence, RI	92
Lawrence B. Hunter	Long Beach, CA	64
Gloria Kosco	Silverdale, PA	147
Denise S. Leone	Hamilton, NY	86
Po Shun Leong	Canoga Park, CA	108
Karen T. Massaro	Santa Cruz, CA	
Alphonse Mattia	Westport, MA	83
Todd E. Noe	Providence, RI	13
Joe Porcelli	Newton, PA	89
Janet Prip	Cranston, RI	110
Mara Superior	Williamsburg, MA	30
Gerald Ulrich	Toledo, OH	17

FURNITURE:

Vered Blatman	Brooklyn, NY	78
Stuart Cohen/Robert Fabielli	Chicago, IL	74
Peter S. Dean	Newton Highlands, MA	69
Lynn DiNino	Philadelphia, PA	
Thomas J. Duffy	Ogdensburg, NY	82
John Dunnigan	W. Kingston, RI	73
John Hein	Trenton, NJ	84
Michael Hurwitz	Philadelphia, PA	68
Bob Ingram/Kathy Halton	Philadelphia, PA	73
Peter Kramer	Washington, VA	77
Gregg Lipton	Portland, ME	13
Daniel Mack	New York, NY	cover
Wendy Maruyama	Berkeley, CA	85
Ronald C. Puckett	Richmond, VA	70
Frederick Puksta	Scottsville, NY	70, 82
Jamie Robertson	Cambridge, MA	76
David L. Smith	North Dartmouth, MA	
Janice C. Smith	Providence, RI	84
Jay Stanger	Charlestown, MA	74
Thomas W. Stender	Boston, NY	68
Howard Werner	Mt. Tremper, NY	82

INSTALLED ARCHITECTURAL ELEMENTS:

Thomas J. Beck	Philadelphia, PA	21
Wayne Brungard	Longmont, CO	154
Gordon S. Bryan	Point Reyes, CA	115
Peter S. Dean	Newton Highlands, MA	150-151
Saara Gallin	White Plains, NY	128
Scott Goewey	Penn Yan, NY	142
Steven Goldner	Bethlehem, PA	145
Lyn Hovey	Cambridge, MA	121
Keith Jellum	Sherwood, OR	111
Ray King	Philadelphia, PA	96
Gloria Kosco	Silverdale, PA	62
Paul Marioni	Seattle, WA	136
Juan and Patricia Navarrete	Taos, NM	14, 143
Narcissus Quagliata	Oakland, CA	131
Judith E. Robertson	Hoboken, NJ	118
Kenneth vonRoenn, Jr.	Louisville, KY	140
Peter Watson	Providence, RI	
Rick Wrigley	Holyoke, MA	142
Larry Zgoda	Chicago, IL	126

NON-FUNCTIONAL DECORATIVE WORK:

Nancy Moore Bess	New York, NY	106
Al Blankschien	Milwaukee, WI	93
Jonathan J. Clowes	Walpole, NH	109
Kathleen Dustin	Reston, VA	104
Christopher R. Ellison	Rochester, NY	110
Kerry Feldman	Marina del Rey, CA	102
Sidney R. Hutter	Jamaica Plains, MA	102
Hyewon Lee	Providence, RI	98
Mary Ann Lomonaco	Larchmont, NY	63
Kira Louscher	Akron, OH	98
Steven Maslach	Greenbrae, CA	102
Thomas McCanna	Woodstock, NY	105
Cynthia Porter	Philadelphia, PA	107
Karyl Sisson	Los Angeles, CA	107
J. Fred Woell	Deer Isle, ME	66

TEXTILES AND FABRICS:

Gloria E. Crouse	Olympia, WA	41
Karen E. Cullen	San Francisco, CA	144
Marion Grant	New York, NY	37
Beth Minear	Washington, DC	44
Martha Donovan Opdahl	Greencastle, IN	41
Sissi Siska	Hoboken, NJ	5
Wendy Wahl	Saunderstown, RI	69-70

JURORS

Brent Brolin, *Architectural Critic and Author*

William Grenewald, *former Executive Director, American Craft Council*

Dorothy Hafner, *Ceramist*

Lloyd E. Herman, *Founding Director, Renwick Gallery, Smithsonian Institution*

Steven Holt, *Product Designer and Writer*

Malcolm Holzman, *FAIA, Architect*

Richard Knapple, *Vice President of Interior Design, Bloomingdale's*

Charles Morris Mount, *Interior Designer*

Albert Paley, *Metalworker*

Ivy Ross, *Designer*

Paul J. Smith, *Director Emeritus, American Craft Museum*

Donna Warner, *Editor, Food and Design, Metropolitan Home*

PHOTO CREDITS

Page	Photographer/Position	Page	Photographer/Position	Page	Photographer/Position
cover	Lynne Reynolds	50	Joe Peoples, *right photos*	105	Courtesy of Paley Studios, *top*
3	Bard Wrisley	52	Suzi Romanik, *top*	106	Len and Joan Weinstock, *bottom*
5	Steve Moore, *top left*	54-55	Peter Sahula	107	Myron Moskwa, *top*
5	Carol Seitz, *bottom left*	56	Gerald Gustafson	107	Tom Brummett, *bottom left*
5	Alex Casler, *bottom right*	57	Bob Wharton, *left*	107	Woody Packard, *bottom right*
6	Daryl J. Bunn	58	Stewart Schwartzberg, *top photos*	108	Frank Wing, *bottom*
10	Langdon Clay, *top*	58	Steve Budman, *bottom*	109	Denis Griggs
10	DeGeus Photographers, *bottom left*	59	Chee-Heng Yeong	109	George Leisey, *inset*
10	William B. Seitz, *bottom center*	60-61	Paul Kivett	110	Roger Birn, *bottom right*
11	John Tanabe	62	Lance Schriner, *bottom*	112	David Lubarsky, *top*
12	Judith Taylor, *top*	63	Rick Albert, *top left*	112	Gary Storm, *bottom left*
12	J.D. Small, *bottom*	63	E.G. Schempf, *top right*	113	Steven Zane
13	John Tanabe, *top*	63	Bob Simons, *bottom*	114	Loveless Photographics
13	James Beards, *bottom*	65	Brian Blauser, *left*	115	William Pelletier, *top*
14	Dan Little	65	Ron Forth, *right*	115	Mel Schockner, *bottom*
15	Paul Warchol, *top*	66	Rick Abrams, *right*	116	Mary Onifer, *top photos*
15	Tom Petrillo, *bottom*	67	Paul G. Beswick	118	Steven Zane
16	Petronella Ytsma, *top left*	68-9	Jim Hedrich, *top*	119	Richard Rodriguez
16	David Wharton, *top right*	68	K.C. Kratt, *bottom left*	120	Martin Berinstein, *bottom*
16	Dave King, *bottom left*	68	Tom Brummett, *bottom right*	121	Alan Oransky
17	Richard Chestnut, *top*	69	Dean Powell	122-123	Alan Oransky
17	Powell Photography, *bottom right*	70	Richard Larimer, *top*	124	Jamie Tuttle, *top*
18-19	Gary Dryden	71	John Tanabe	124	Larry Thall, *bottom*
20	Daryl J. Bunn, *bottom*	72	Jackson Hill, *top*	125	Brett Froomer
22-23	Hollis Officer, *top*	72	Lester Sullivan, *bottom*	126	Alan Oransky, *top*
23	Ralph Gabriner	73	Tom Brummett, *bottom photos*	126	Tom Sawyer, *bottom left*
24	Richard Rodriguez, *top*	74	Jim Hedrich, *top*	126	Christopher Kean, *bottom right*
24	Tom Weigand, *bottom*	74	Steve Greenway, *bottom left*	127	Mr. and Mrs. John Pillsbury, Jr.
25	Dawn Doga, *top*	74	Dean Powell, *bottom right*	128	Leland Cook, *top*
25	Paul Schraub, *bottom photos*	76	Leo Gozbekian	128	Frank Baptie, *bottom*
26-27	Bob Michels	77	Powell Photography, *bottom*	129	Frank Baptie
28	Tom Mills, *top photos*	79	Paul Warchol	130	Bruce Fritz
28	Rick Patrick, *middle*	80-81	Elliot Fine	131	Bill Kane
28	Daryl J. Bunn, *bottom and inset*	82	Woody Packard, *bottom right*	132-133	Gary Hall
29	David Palmer	83	Powell Photography, *top left*	134	Bill Kane
30	Susie Cushner, *top*	83	Kip Brundage, *bottom left*	135	James Wilson
32	Fred Weiss, *top*	85	Dean Powell, *left, top right*	136	Jake Seniuk
32	Baker Vail, *bottom*	85	Gary Okazaki, *right middle, bottom*	137	J.D. Small
33	Lynn Hamrick, *top right*	86	Alan Oransky, *top*	139	Mike Partenio
34	David Keister	86	Richard Walker, *bottom left*	140	Richard Walker, *left, top and center*
35	Jeffrey Sabo	86	Gary/Suzi, *bottom right*	140	Barry Halprin, *top right*
36	Frank Poole, *top*	87	Ron Forth	140	Quadrant, *bottom*
36	Shrimpton Photography, *middle*	88	Kip Brundage, *left*	141	Kerry Carruth
36	Hollis Officer, *bottom left*	88	Daryl J. Bunn, *right*	142	Dan Little, *top*
36	Hugh Tifft, *bottom center/right*	89	Michael D'Orio, *top left*	142	Michael Burnett, *bottom left*
37	E.Z. Smith, *top photos*	89	James Beards, *top right*	142	Michael Janeszek, *bottom right*
37	Fred Weis, *center*	89	Charles Mayer, *bottom photos*	144	Baker Vail, *bottom*
37	Gordon Holland, *bottom*	90-91	Tom Petrillo	145	Eugene Mopsik
38	Mark Green, *top*	93	John Harvey, *left*	146	Bruce Fritz
39	Mark Green	93	Alan Linn, *right*	147	Bruce Fritz, *bottom*
40	Jack Parsons	94	Swain Edens, *top, bottom left*	148	Alan Oransky
41	Pierson Photographics, *bottom*	94	Lester Lefkowitz, *right*	149	William B. Seitz
42	Pat Ripp, *bottom photos*	95	Mehosh Dziadzio	150	Morse/Peterson Photographers
43	Gary L. Warnimount	96	Robert Grove	151	Morse/Peterson Photographers
44	Edward Owen, *top*	97	Terrance Shukle	152	Suzi Romanik
44	Bruce Miller, *bottom photos*	98	J. Dean, *top*	153	Blake Praytor, *bottom left*
45	Gary Dryden, *top and right*	99	Duncan Johnson	153	Dennis Geaney, *bottom right*
46-47	Gordon Beall	100-101	Alan Watson	154	Lee Milne
49	David Heinlein	102	John Forsman, *bottom left*		
50	Barry Pribula, *left photos*	102	Charles Mayer, *bottom right*		
		103	Anthony Potter		
		104	Richard Rodriguez, *top photos*		
		104	Dawn Doga, *bottom photos*		

ACKNOWLEDGMENTS

THIS BOOK IS A COLLABORATION. IT IS, OF COURSE, WRITTEN AND edited and designed, but the heart and soul of the book is the work done by the artists. Without their skills and their enthusiastic support for the project, there would be no book.

We also are indebted to the owners of much of the work who permitted us to show the crafts in place and at work in their homes.

And, of course, Lisa Govan, who took all of these pictures and words and made a coherent, stunning whole of them.